THE CYCLIC VARIATIONS

and more new poems

THE CYCLIC VARIATIONS

and more new poems

Alastair Macdonald

NEWFOUNDLAND POETRY SERIES

BREAKWATER

BREAKWATER BOOKS LIMITED
100 Water Street • P.O. Box 2188
St. John's, NL • A1C 6E6
www.breakwaterbooks.com

Library and Archives Canada Cataloguing in Publication

Macdonald, Alastair
    The cyclic variations and more new poems / Alastair Macdonald.

(Newfoundland poetry series)
ISBN 978-1-55081-238-1

    I. Title. II. Series.

PS8575.D6C93 2007   C811'.54   C2007-900778-3

© 2007 Alastair Macdonald

Author Photograph: Ruth Lawrence

We acknowledge the financial support of The Canada
Council for the Arts for our publishing activities.

We acknowledge the support of the Department of
Tourism, Culture and Recreation for our publishing
activities.

Canadä

We acknowledge the financial support of the
Government of Canada through the Book Publishing
Industry Development Program (BPIDP) for our
publishing activities.

Printed in Canada.

To my friends in Newfoundland

ACKNOWLEDGEMENTS

THE CYCLIC VARIATIONS

Certain variations from this cycle were published as
separate poems (provided with titles) before the
year-long-plus sequence was accomplished (*TickleAce*,
Nos. 31, 39.) A condensed five-variation preview of the
complete work (without titles to poems) was published
in *TickleAce*, No. 33. One or two other variations (with
titles) were published in The *Newfoundland Quarterly*, and
in the anthology *Voices from the Rock*, Selected and Edited
by Everard H. King, Harry Cuff Publications, St. John's,
2000. Titles temporarily applied to individual variations,
so published, have now been removed. They are replaced
by the uniform and less distracting order of small
Roman numerals. This is a more desirably neutral mode
of identification for the components of the sequence,
and allows each variation to speak directly for itself.

MORE NEW POEMS

Five recent poems have been published in *The Aberdeen
University Review* (U.K.), Spring, 2004, pp. 240-42:
'The Ahbutster', 'Fall Dusk', 'Entertaining Couples',
'The Sunshine on the Road', 'In the Park'. The poem
'Verses' was published with an accompanying cartoon

drawing in *The Newfoundland Quarterly*, Vol. 91, No. 1, 2005, pp. 29. These poems are included in the MORE NEW POEMS section of this book.

The cover is a cartoon, 'Spring Woods', one of several dozen cartoons that Alastair created over the years.

Acknowledgements are given to the above publications and their editors, with gratitude for acceptance of my work over many years.

My thanks also to Dr. Helen Peters of Memorial University for her sustained interest, and helpful advice.

Thank you to Vanessa Stockley and Todd Manning. These two friends have been very helpful with proof reading of the book, and generally keping an eye on things.

And once again I am happy to have benefited from the computer services of Veronica LeGrow, with whose technical skills and accuracy I was already familiar.

For Clyde Rose and Breakwater Books, again my gratitude and praise for their careful and tasteful productions of many of my poetry collections.

CONTENTS

THE CYCLIC VARIATIONS

☾

MORE NEW POEMS

The Cyclic Variations
of a Newfoundland year

THE CYCLIC VARIATIONS
Of a Newfoundland Year

The theme is this place, and the turning year,
its opening fulfilment and decline,
and nature's showings in its fluid schemes
for confluences blendings partings, where,
from this small point of vision of just one
contained perception which reports a real
to us, we try, placed as we now are here
in looking out, and up, around, to find
meaning within the fired emotions' sun.
And from the many reals of sciences
philosophies and arts engaging mind
with claims to show the truth of what we are,
we may well look to our own view at last
from which to shape what may be caught, held fast.

Var. i

The lake stares
in its setting of wavy ground
with grass, low tree and bush.
The water is now a gleaming grey
like freshly sliced lead

feathered by a breeze,
or blued steel,
under a windy sun.
The trees are pushed
by the prevailing blow
to a fixed slant.
From the shores
some birds fly up
at intervals in their
unending quest for sustenance,
never since chickhood
laid on,
stacked in some handy bird-fridge.

Var. ii

The shore is edged by trees,
from their start, bent
one way by the constant winds,
like old old people,
everlastingly.

So it has been for some,
and with no chance
of another way:
to stand upright,
now shift to glimpse a passer-by,
face sunset and the climbing dawn,
or wave sometimes
out to sea.

Var. iii

Leafless quiet. A waiting.
The northern world waiting.
Waiting for the not far
winter solstice.
Waiting for the lengthening days,
the storms, the snow, the gales,
the spring.
A metamorphosis,
like the rest.
But season in itself too,
though we may disown,
as we try to wait it out,
see its spare beauty
of windless calm, clear skies,
sun pale as watercolour wash,

suffusing all with slanted light.
In it we see
the already longed-for spring,
a summer again,
to this again, unable to grasp, hold
each again, watching them pass,
waiting for death,
for life again.

Var. iv

The snow is driven in bands
parallel to the ground,
in horizontal wind-borne waves.
A single crow flies with them
in swift and bounced perplexity.
Snow falls and blows,
suspending routines of life
as if all were to end here
in the white howl. A car is stuck
in a bank of drift. On foot
the driver battles off.
Diaphanous scarves of snow
skim the blown-bare ground
in desperate, meaningless chase.
Then, after a length, all stops.

Next day the world is visible again,
lies calm, as features, sharp and clear, advance
on the smiling as if apologetic
face of the stilled white:
half-opened fans of the black trees,
the red or green of a house or barn.
Leafless bush, stalk, shoot emerge,
a strange and grey-brown fuzz
against the snow, wondering
to what, to where
it should belong.
In the sun from the gold-blue sky
tree shadows spread across
the brushed and hard-ridged seas of snow
as elongated feathers, lilac, blue,
which glide up, over, down the rises,
furrows, hollows, valleys, cliffs,
the scores and whorls of the wind's
hands and footprints on the snow.

Var. v

The lake is ice.
It holds mirrored things
almost as still water,
but hazily,
as under gauze.

The ice is like glazed and humpy water.
The sun, as on water, marches
in its long reflected band of light
under a glacial wind that whips
the brown dead grass,
the beaten shrubs.
On the streaky grey-white ice
grey gulls hunch and crouch,
compressed into a tight pack,
each compressed into itself,
waiting, it seems,
for the cold's death.

Var. vi

About the lake the snow lies,
flat, or heaved in gentle curves
with the upcast ground.
Objects are dark on the white, a fir
green-black, the brownish smudge
of leafless tree or bush, a hut,
some houses clustering. In far
and miniature silhouette
a man and his leashed dog.
With saintly patience he will stop
seconds to seconds and allow

his charge to sniff and then dispense
its endless-seeming spargings as
the marks of territory.
Air is sharp, scent clean from the cold.
Above, a low sun is compressed
into a flat and clear-cut disc, pale
buff, with merest strawberry blush
through frosty haze. The lake is now
frozen to safe depth, powdered white,
with muffled figures, sexless and
darkly blocked. The adult skaters
slanted at a forward angle
glide and swoop, blades etching ice
with hissed caress, in mastery look-
at-me exultant. Tiny tots
skate just steps to laughing tumbles.
Vast, a Newfoundland black dog, young,
playful with slow bounds and gambols,
fur jet and soft and blowable
as soot, is with a woman, man,
and child. It lollops after them
as they skate, but now and then,
massively friendly yet aloof,
heads off to join some other crowd:
as boys with hockey sticks, and puck
it would like to catch but is not
fast enough. It runs and leaps
in near-arrested motion in the air,

as in a film slowed. Sometimes
it comes ashore but soon goes back
to the ice. To find its owners,
shadow again the hockey lads,
enjoy the easier smoothness
of this less familiar surface,
sweet, and also cooling to the paws?

All this activity above,
as the sun glows strawberry now,
sinking towards a turquoise band
of sky which brushes the land's edge,
as time seems to wait
under the snow.
Days more and the ice will soften.
Skaters will be gone, while the gulls
alight to repossess their lakedom.

Var. vii

Melting sheet ice on the water
floats in patches on the water
like the clouds in the sky
reflected in the water.
Cloud and ice blend in the water
with the cold sky,
blue in the frigid light.

Var. viii

Here the spring is late, as if
the grudging land, wedded to
the eternal bridegroom winter,
said, This is no country for you
of southern romantic dreaming.
We make some small concessions, but...
Above and through the trees, still bare,
the sky is a cross-hatched, sometimes
luminous dough,
or as soiled linen, long unwashed.
Birds are twittering, even. Gulls
descend, then squat, fly off again.
They chatter, chunter, squawk, and tear
from themselves the same insistent notes
jarringly screeched,
in practice of mating preludes.
Air will sometimes waft
elusive scentings of a spring
from well beyond. Somewhere always
the spring is late, trailing a sense
that we are too, with something missed.
In time it will come here, but then
the ideal summer of elsewhere
is leaving soon. Now we are in
the long long spell of waiting, grey
as the sky, recurrent squalls, the snow.
March and April fade
to May with little change.

The waiting is far drawn. Too far
for not a season.
The bridegroom has stepped outside.
Though I've clutched and tried
to hold him, says the land,
he must go for a while.
But not for long. Oh, not for long.

Var. ix

The rain is washing away
the snow that covered us.
Through the white, stalks and grass
rise from pits at the root.
Patches and ridges of ground,
islets and parings of lawn
emerge, yellow-brown
with touches of green.
Trees and branches lose
definition lent by the snow
and merge into the blur,
neutrality of one another.
Rain is washing the snow away
easing the hold of winter dormancy.

The earth is appearing,
drying. Roads will soon

be clean and bare,
leading far
by field and over down
into the spring.
Smoke sharpens air
with acrid stimulus.
And straw will blow
about. Young leaves will show
with wheeling birds
and clouds against the blue
and sun on water quivering.

Another set of aims reviving
with the cycle of necessity.
Not that there seems for us
a special promise here:
only joy if we can share
in this fresh impulse of the year
from nature's strategy.
Except for something different:
with us there is an end to it.

Var. x

The wind is brisk,
with bustling force,
the lake a glinting sheet
harrowed by whipping gusts.
The clouds are woolly rounds,
soft, grey with white above.
They move on a firm shell
of duck-egg blue.
Sun splashes down some green and gold
with darks, making the view
keen-edged, salient.
Skied high, buffeted, birds veer.
Shadows from the clouds in motion
fly in gliding cling
to contours of the land.
Old grass burning far away
tangs the stirring air
with the ache for what's past,
what yet may be.
Nature is busy about
its cyclic process.
Part of this, we feel the surge
of energy and aim.

Var. xi

The hold is loosening.
Tips of trees and bushes are
now tinted reddish-brown
and yellow, pink
as the buds yield.
Here and there some now tuft out
with fan-like starts of leaves.
Tasselled catkins swing, and mark
the air's imperceptible stir.
Water and sky are the same
cleansed blue. Spring is seen
coming over the fields
misting woods and hedges
with emergent green.
Shadows of tree branches,
grey or faintest mauve, now reach
and softly finger walls, bare boles
of other trees, stretch far
over emerald pastures,
seeming to point to that
beyond themselves youth,
with them, thought
it saw.

Var. xii

Full summer now and the leafed trees
move like blown ships across the land.
The sails of their foliage stream
and the long grasses flow like silk
undulate to the wind's surge.
Summer is come. Like the visitation,
on her clock-tight day, of a reigning queen,
soon perforce to leave, it brings
disruption, change, excitement, and
discomfort unavowed.
But we can pretend that summer's long.
From dandelion yellow to the blueberry
when the wind falls the time
can weigh leaden with heat.
Above the land's fringe the sky
shines a luminous grey-blue,
darkening towards the zenith
to nearly the black of space.
Or it is all the deepest blue,
and clouds are islands,
motionless cushions of down,
soft white to palest peach,
their outlines gently brushed into the blue;
or harder edged with a painted-on, Chirico look,
contours unnaturally smooth
and yet contorted, convoluted,

seeming to demand attention then
proclaim, protest or challenge, mock.
Flies mass in dancing clumps.
Bees hum, and shadows are black.
A circling grove cradles a pool,
the whole in richest shade
as if waiting for a Gainsborough to add
the patient heat-stilled cows or market cart.
The old embrace the warmth, or complain.
In the hot dusks from villages and towns,
by meadows, youths and girls are on the move,
along the streets, on foot, by cycle, car,
in search of one another, the new life
the beckoning tall year seems to pledge
in this heightened drive for love.

Var. xiii

Long grasses. In July
they gain full height.
Across the water, edging it,
they're seen to rise
like walls of fur or hair,
green, upright, motionless
in summer heat,
brightened with blue vetch,

buttercups, the clover
red and white,
or sweeping low, depressed
by rain-soaked winds,
to resurrect themselves in sun.
They border the lake's path,
high as well-grown hedges,
as concealing, though
a fluid, gale-tossed,
shifting, parting screen,
bowing in waves
before the gusts
like heads of shining hair.
Tall as adult people,
they reveal
only the moving faces
of the walkers-by.
The flowering peaked crowns,
engendering seed,
from their rat-tail starts
have opened into
feathery flummery,
rose pink, grey, pale lime,
washed ochre, yellow, brown;
and shorter grasses
which remain
their rat-tail, cat-tail green.

Not in the frame, the terms,
of nature and its sciences
they've achieved life
to change, to shelter, hide,
to make the look
of summer different,
bring mystery, beauty,
veil and soften
winter's rigid line.

Var. xiv

Jockeying winds race-whip the waves
hissing to shore.
From laved, bright-glinting stones
necklaced with driven spume,
at a fresh turn of the lake,
astonishing,
the sudden thrusts
of irises
rear tall, guardsmen-erect,
like a bold command,
sun-yellow as today's hope,
like a shout for joy.

Var. xv

Five o'clock this July morning.
The level sun is bright, and cool
through air rinsed fresh by dews.
The early morning gleam is like
stage lighting, angled and phantom,
low, skimming the land.
On the ground
lie massed, flat walls of shade,
windowed in gold.
The garden lengthens, empty yet
of people and event.
From orchard trees the shadows,
with the dew to slip away
by noon's hot glare,
spread over and beyond a seat,
drawn out with those
of the tall, house chimneys,
over the lawns,
long
as our lengthening day
waiting to be filled.

Var. xvi

The cooling, heat-engendered breeze
lifts the curtains of today,
as in memory
along the enfilade
of rooms at a childhood home,
the white and gauzy draperies of July
would billow in, like sails ballooning.

From the garden
they floated the warm stillness,
the hum of bees on the hypericum,
unpuzzled confidence of safety, love,
the sense that there was always much to be,
to do, for long long long and far ahead,
and that all time would be ours to fill.

Var. xvii

Windsurfing.
The laborious setting up.
The clamber and wet balancing.
The manoeuvring to catch
with the right slant
the rogue, nose-stopping wind.
And then (can it be true)
the flight before the blow —
the fused poise

(to the watcher),
like a bird
or insect bright
with unlikely tint,
of human, board, and sail
at fish-fin angle.
The skim on water
(endless-seeming run)
like a yacht but finer,
frail, more delicately spun.

And with no warning the
collapse again,
and the doused tangle.

Var. xviii

The wind storms.
For days and nights
its pressure is sustained,
injects leaf-loaded trees
with violent life.
They may have loved it at first,
the change from July somnolence,
from rest on the black rounds
of their deep midsummer shade.
Moving again at last,
coursing away and far
over hills and pastures,
chasing the clouds' shadows,
scudding with them for some need,
achievement, ecstasy.
The trees are youth itself.
They're a racing of horses
with the stretching manes;
are waves combing surfaces of seas
or fields of undulant grasses;
streams of long-haired girls
speeding to their lovers;
wild-locked Maenads
frenzied for their god.
Though not departing from their sites
they're travelling with all the world
in covered distances, believing
it takes journeying to find

what we desire to find
or that which may be found
elsewhere, not here.

Then all is calm again.
On the grass the debris of
commotion, severed leaves
in their still live green, from broken
twigs to the whole branch, augers
of autumn's sidle, not quite near.
And now blow stronger gusts
and lashing rains,
with sudden blastings, beat, and swish
pasting soaked leaves on windows' glass.
Let slip are the dogs of wind,
attacking trees, massed woodlands even,
growling, worrying, convulsing,
tossing, rending violently.
In the gale's force and swirls
the clothed trees writhe and twist,
straining to fly, move with the power
that wrestles to unseat, to gather them
along to the somewhere, nowhere
rushed to. Flying in all but
forward movement, they respond
and gesture only in
their torment, rooted fast.

Later, storms of the fall
will strike with harsher rain
as whips to lash the winds,
trees then waning gaunt, on
to another phase.

Var. xix

When our infancy was in green places
without knowing it we early knew
flickers of sun through leaves,
the dazzle of day on rivers,
lamplit autumn windows
trembling through screens
of windy branches,
shimmer, quiver, rustle, glint,
the long pulsating sigh of moving air
through sounding trees in summer,
winter's dry crack and whip
of the bare boughs,
the pressured rivulets of birdsong
in springtime's cleansing wash
of yielding dewy buds,
the hot dry bite of sunshine.
And because we knew them then
we respond still to these things,

which still are, thinking every time
it is a yes which is of now,
starting new fervours, ferments,
knowing and unaware it is
the then in now which leaps out,
the old sensations — beguiling,
seeming to promise, urging belief
that self's completeness can be won —
dreams which have pointed and led,
and have brought us
to here.

Var. xx

Late summer, on autumn's edge.
The leaves green yet,
but curled and tired.
A wet day. No rain,
but it has rained.
The grass underfoot, wet.
The rhododendron clumps
in the shrubberies drip.
The shield-shaped lake, heraldic,
has for its mantling
swirls of mist.
A solitary bird sings, in hopefulness,

as we might choose to say.
The scents and sounds of wetness
saturate the spirit,
weigh it down,
as if the days would not
dry bright with warmth and joy again,
as they will, and so
perpetuate this alternation.

Var. xxi

The lake is glass in this September sun.
Trees and bushes on its shores,
an angler's hut, hang down, inverted,
whole, defined,
blurred only by a crinkling
from the water's unseen flow.
Around them clouds from the sky
float, puff-balls of grey
with hints of rose and lemon
on the turquoise blue.
The trees stand upright, motionless.
On bush and brushwood
autumn's gossamer filaments
gleam as they wire the twigs
and yellowing leaves for touch.

The tang of growth's decay is
in these early stages sweet,
evocative of nameless things
long lost, the resumed school times,
the half-remembered what and when.
The haws shine scarlet in the hedge.
At night the moon astonishes in gold,
entrancing with its charge of hope
for dreams, desires.

Var. xxii

The sky is overcast, with smoky cloud
hiding the sun. Patches of blue show.
The afternoon is darkening even at five,
brings thoughts of longer nights, in weeks
the clocks set back that hour.
The winds are a soft balm
this late September day. They blow
remembrances of, where crops
are barley wheat and rye,
harvests done and fields of stubble calm,
rosy in sunny light before the plough
makes brown those fields of turned earth
ready for winter seeding, far away
in years as well as place. When children

have gone back to school, fervid
and zesty from new challenges,
impatient for all that time ahead
to roll towards them. Hurry. Time is slow.
Can one remember that,
this melancholy, gentle afternoon,
hear those voices, see the stubble fields,
the berried hedges dream to Hallowe'en,
Christmas beyond, bright in this season
of expectancy, young energy,
activity restored by summer light.

Var. xxiii

October gold.
The lake gleams. Grasses still high,
fringe to its shores, shine pale pale blond
in their decay. The trees' gold appears
to suffuse the air with gold,
the sunlit air the leaves. The wind is strong
and cool, the sky cerulean blue.
Above the earth's rim banks of cloud
stand white, like a mountain range
of sunlit snow. Behind the golden leaves
and light, winter proclaims itself
in subtle overlapping change

of season and effects. Smoothly, it seems,
nature fulfils constrained functional musts
without question or concern, quite unaware
of our response, and not like us
compelled to ask, explain, object.

Var. xxiv

An autumn gale.
October rain
streams down the window-glass.
Outside the woodlands struggle,
lash this way and that
in waves of gamboge hue
and cadmium red.
Their frail grip broken
leaves fly up the troubled sky,
sheer off, away. Green ground
is starred with fallen ones,
bright still as gold,
but in bewilderment —
so violently displaced
by twist and tear.
Mist clouds the middle air.
The sky is low
and packed with grey

fast-moving yeast
and glinting murk
above the brown
and hurrying lake.
The water charges to the shore,
as flying riders proud
and plumed with ivory foam,
to die as nothing
on the beach of stones.
Next day will see
a change, a farther step
from summer's close:
the foliage thinned,
the underlying nakedness
of bush and tree
exposed.

Var. xxv

The sky fills itself.
What seems its inverted bowl
enclosing us holds nothing but
its blue, darkening overhead,
and paler azure, luminous
where its curve descends to fit
the horizons circling round,
with hints of yellow there.
The sun stands unassertively,
unseen behind its veiling light,
but fills the air with gilded motes
which shimmer, animate the blue.
Objects are sharp. At a point
above the land's verge, barely clearing it,
are narrow smears, grey charcoal marks
not readily perceptible.
They're vapour, hardly formed as cloud.
They will not move, rise, build, possess
the sky. Today's day is not theirs
to assert a presence. Quietly,
before one looks again, they'll go.

Another day
the clouds are large and widely spaced,
irregularly round and lumpish,
soft as plumped up pillows,
overboldly three-dimensional
like those which burst from canvases

in paintings, amateur,
the primitives; cold grey beneath,
above, where the light sculpts,
touched sweeteningly with faint caress
of primrose, peach, on Day-Glo white.
A late season's travesty, it seems,
of summer's snowy upthrust palaces,
serenely cool and pure
above earth-level heat.
This day's are not seen to move, although
down here a late October wind
strains, forcible and chill, among the trees
now almost stripped of gold,
above the rippled, iron lake,
dark blue, in places blinding
from the sun's flash.

Or again,
in gales clouds race.
Across the blank, wide air,
as driven by desperate aim,
in unremitting haste they flee,
grey, ragged, fraying,
momentarily coalescing,
massing, as fast breaking thin,
like smoke from phantom worlds on fire,
unthinkably far off.

It does not close, this endless running show.
Their set piece, stationary groupings, their
sensational processions do not flag.
Programmed to give distraction and
indifferent to our wonder, awe, indifference,
these skyey players strut and fret, dissolve,
to be perpetually renewed.
Their stores of properties, effects,
rich and diverse as worlds, and aeons old,
are inexhaustible. Shows must go on.
Pale, gentle fleeces; storm-black billows, racks,
against metallic gleams or smouldering reds;
flame, darkness, blood are staged, and conjure with
the affections of some watchers here,
believers, or victims of illusion's play.

And then at nights the moon,
bereft of mysteries, old hat rock
which should know better, scampers, chases with
the blue-lit curds of clouds, trailing its lures —
the hope for knowledge, opportunity,
fulfilment and romance — to prompt, entice
the yearning, upward gaze below.

Var. xxvi

When sheathing husks of now dead leaves
are blown away, there is before
November's end a second spring
in the budding and opening of rose,
brown, yellow brick, the rust
of roof-tiles, chimney-pots,
cobalt of slate;
the forms of emergent housing —
shoebox, cube, long ranch, high-rise,
unfolding of walls, straights, angles;
flowerings, green, puce, black
of garden tool – and potting-sheds;
the burgeoning of paths and contours
of the ground; the white of
post-and-rail round paddocks, fields,
the golden light of sun
off window-glass; the sharp
and upward growth of towers and spires;
uncurling, of the street-lamp stalks;
massed-bluebell misty blue on fragile mesh
of chain-link fences. Evergreens —
cypress, holly, yew, spruce, pine
come out again. And there's the look
of chocolate, buff, and azure distance
through transparent scrims of trees.
The purity of line, dormant,
unseen, and waiting out
the summer's winter, stands revealed
in the pale sunburst of a world
reborn.

Var. xxvii

The wind seethes. The lake, dun,
is travelling fast. Waves leap.
The trees, bent over, cower
before the blast, ripped nearly stark,
leaves whisked with summer and then
the autumn's hues to nowhere.
Drifts of the fallen rattle, scrunch.
Gulls mewl and totter in the air.
The sky is flat grey tin, a lid
clamped down, tight-lipped as if
in rueful disavowal,
sour acceptance of the change.

Var. xxviii

The trees are bare now,
black inked nets against
the sky's cold blue.
A shrivelled leaf,
besieged pockets of leaves
hold out yet in the lost war,
noticed not, or but
as lingering blemishes
on the flowered and pure
victorious filigrees. The green
massed forces of each summer,
conquering, hiding all, concede
to the skeleton, which lasts
longer.

Var. xxix

The grey November sky is matt as felt,
scrolled beneath by darker whirls
of blackish cloud. Above the land's end
gleams a lurid slash. The water
is pewter-dull except when the sun
bursts through and spears across the lake
in a band unnaturally bright,
as the jarring metallic flare
from a hologram print.
There is rain in the gusts.
Trees and bushes bend and stream,
outstripped by their stripping withered scraps.
The ducks move hopefully still
in their mild, uncertain-seeming quests,
trailing their chevron wakes.
Pressed down by the sky's stilled turbulence,
the light sears, in Götterdämmerung blaze.
It is taking its leave, along with summer.
Ahead is the time of lamplight,
warmth indoors and safety, once
in the younger days looked forward to
for Christmas joys, the gifts, the clean page
of a new year.

Var. xxx

In this hiatus which is December
the month seems unsure
what nature is about,
the summer swept away on the winds,
trees stripped, the winter not yet come,
no longer warm and yet not cold.
The winds seem left from something, somewhere,
the equinox, last hurricanes far south;
like lost ghosts seem doubtfully to wander
with neither force nor feeble stir
but strong enough to agitate
the bare black webs of trees
against the mornings' angry skies, rose-flamed.
Birds wing the light,
now singly, now in flocks,
to themselves perhaps with meaningful intent,
but purposeful about
they may know not what.
High up there must be stronger wind.
The blood-tinged morning clouds
have a curving, up-brushed look.
There is a feeling of suspension,
in phenomena a betokening,
as the year runs as if released
towards the piling and the climax
of the mounting, whelming dark,

the shortest day, first and the only
longest night this cycle,
stasis and the turning, the fresh start
of the winter solstice.
The lake rests in stillness, now enclosed
by its dead reeds and grasses,
looking to its past year
now largely sunk from view,
the summer lily pads,
the water-fringing irises,
even the last berries, lately red
on bush and tree, lost to the birds and winds.
All that outside, beyond, happened, happening,
receiving our unsought attention, seeming to imply
meaning, without intending it, or being aware.
Small children now descend on their local school,
on foot, or dropped from cars.
Instinctively, excitedly, they know
elation in these heady, flagrant dawns
which fire with thoughts of work and play,
the holidays now close, another year
of their so many more, a *new*
year, which, as it ever seems,
deserves their hope and trust,
and is to bring all happiness.

More new poems

THE FIRST OF MAY
A Pastoral

Half asleep,
so far unbreakfasted,
a small crowd, we sat in punts
on the flowery, blossomy
first of May
we assumed to be there,
closed off by walls of early mist.
Chilled, damply we were afloat
on course for Magdalen
to hear the Carol
wafting up, down
from the high tower.
Romantic
said to be
in the empty dawn.
Something done perhaps once
while you are there,
or not at all.
In the daybreak raw and grey
we hunched over portable stoves
in the temporarily moored
and waggling punts.
A girl (beautiful, casting spells)
was mistressminding
punt-borne us and breakfast,
a Zuleika Dobson of my time.

She was also, then, the girlfriend
of a man I knew, but that seemed
to be losing fervour
though not over, and I basked
in auras of attraction
I suppressed,
loath to nurture
treacherous love,
although not yet in thrall.
A mildly muddied Cherwell of a stream.
Somehow it would run clear.
Meantime but a scent,
a colouring, fragrant, roseate,
fingering my consciousness.
Hunger appeased,
we punted on to Magdalen.
Heard the Carol chime.

All that was over early.
Hours yet to the proper day
that would seem
another day,
when I was with a different group.
Oxford affords you circles.
Unlike the Olympics' rings
they need not interlace.
In any one you are at ease.

Morning had broken,
sun-washed, glorious.
All day it would become
a first of summer days.
An uncle-patron of a friend
was visiting,
requiring honour, entertainment.
We had rallied. Some had cars
and we drove to Minster Lovell,
on to Bicester, Banbury, and Burford,
stopped where we would,
to stretch, to look, eat, drink, repose
in unbroken sun or leafy shades.
And talked out, rested, cooled, bestirred,
at five we'd set off back
by main roads, risked detours,
through the green proximities
towards distances of smoky blue,
to be in Oxford streets again.
Some had their evening plans.
My friend took his uncle and a few of us
to dine as guests in his college hall.
And after, northwards to The Trout,
as the long sun sloped down Cumnor way,
for drink and talk in the crowded scene
on the terrace by the rushing weir,
to dusking evening's water scents.

That start of May had been
a festival of young companionship
when our rest-of-lives raced out there
in a world of seeming possibles.
We'd answered the lure of movement
across landscapes of the ground,
the mind, the spirit,
managing then as best we could
(with hope, and sometimes even happiness)
our phase of life,
in a place of beauty at a time
when the time was right,
and the future, drawing us to it,
seemed not now,
and if momentarily glimpsed that day
only as a golden haze.

The enlivening but uneasy thoughts of love
kept drifting through my hours
even while I'd willingly embraced,
as at that age we generously can,
the thoughts, concerns of others.
And my own cross of conscience
event might yet relieve.

A whole day,
rounded, globe-like
in the memory, and
inviolable now.

THE SUNSHINE ON THE ROAD

In evening's day-warmed hour
when he could venture out
and take a few steps, hesitant,
there came a surge of feeling
from sixty years before:
he walking between hedges
where hawthorn blossom snowed,
in strong and morning brilliance
and sunshine on the road;
long from his back his shadow,
shortening, darkly inked,
and the way stretching, enticing,
to where he was making for,
his step elastic, buoyant,
to find which aims could be.
What then was the occasion
he could not now have told,
but lived still the sensation,
even with powers much failed,
of his once young time springing there,
and purpose firm in hope that day,
the outset of a going
which had led from far to where.

READING FICTION

The novel is nearly done:
just a few chapters to go.
Though we spin them out
the end is in sight
of society known
for many days now.

An imagined world has possessed
us, more real than the life
we're in; of meaning, finite,
its pattern complete.
Yet it still will invest
with its aura the actual we're of

for a few days more.
We've been in love with it,
or ourselves in it, and the end
is broken fantasy,
hiatus of vacancy.
Oh, at what hour
does the library shut?

VERSES

To Celebrate The Time Of The Electronic Clock.

The Author Having Many Such Pieces Set About
Each Of His Chambers.

(May Be Sung To Mr. George Frederick Handel's Air
For Lines Of Mr. Pope's Pastoral, 'Summer'.)

Where-e'er you look, smart Clocks pinpoint the Hour,
Time, where you sit, shall permeate your Bow'r,
When Glances dart, shall quail not at your Glow'r
(While Batt'ries last). Though sequent Moments try,
With stealthy Shift, to slip unnoticed by,
Awareness' Lapse their Onward cannot hide,
With such Recording Angels clicking at your Side.

ON SEEING MRS. MARGARET SMITH COURT, SPECTATOR, AUSTRALIA'S OPEN, 2005.

Twistings, furrowings,
curlings of the flesh
at first glimpse
suggest a gravity.
A legend now,
of known benevolence,
with skin tan-hued
as her head in bronze
above the courts at Melbourne.
Character, event
have worked the face
in some agreement with
the underlying bone.
Criss-crossing lines
have traced what's passed.
Criss-cross her racquet flashed
with managed holds
and sure control
of aim and placement, force,
to gain those many championships.

Older today, she wears her aura
of a kindly dignity and power.
Undoubted personage,
impressive, even if
not all know who.

And then at a miracle return
Serena Williams hurls,
the sweetness of the smile,
the recollected joy,
the youth again
that salves
the unremitting years.

ENTERTAINING COUPLES

Don't you love couples?
The Hubers, The Wranglinghams,
The Swizzlestickses?
Shall we have them in to dine?

More testing are the married who
insistently retain pre-nuptial names:
The Edward Paltring — and Sally Farquins,
The Crispin Dax-Gormley — and Jane Doleses.
And WBCs now itemly housed,
for how long who can say.

With flurries of exclamatory hails
drinks are reached, words can't be found
to extol eventual food.
Later talking has its risks.
Agree with one against the other and
you trap looks interchanged,
learn which subjects are not safe.

And then 'Beware the Jabberwock'
of cross-attractions'
'jaws that bite, the claws that catch!',

in case tonight's not ended with tonight.

PUSSY

does not

like being

brushed stand

still even

with the

fine wire

brush which

jerks the

knots in

her long fur and makes it

flow like water through a weir

miaow

AN AGE OF INNOCENCE

Itll soon be time
for back to school
something I dont want
to think about — not yet.
I like school on the whole.
Therar always boys,
some masters too,
whore stinkers, tho usully
more are decent ones.
Were certain to have
to write a piece
'What I Did in the Holidays'
'My Best Times in the Holidays'
'How I Spent the Month of Awgust'
'Why it was Easy to Forgett School
These Hols'. Ha Ha! Titles
just like that.
Instead of waiting to have it
sprung on you the first days back
Ill think (a bit) about it now
and jot down thots
I can praps use.
Im writeing it all in
Modern Poyetry.
Iv looked examples
up in books —
no riming words,
short lines, and this
is what its like.

My Father he keeps bees,
twenty or thirty hives.
Theyre in part of The Gardens
called The Apiary. Its too near
The Orchard, where I like to be
for cherrys, gooseberrys, appels,
plums in summertime.
Offen I get stung.
Dad why do we have bees —
so very <u>many</u> bees?
It's just a recreation.
Whats a rek reeation dad?
Something you like to do
that you don't have to,
he said, like Mycroft.
What is my croft dad —
a bit of your land?
Oh, man in a story
you'll get to know
before too long.

I said that I got stung.
One right on my forehead
swelled all down
to close my eyes
and I was BLIND
for THREE WHOLE DAYS.
Id just to lie
in a darkend room.

Why the room had to
be darken when
I coudnt see
I do not know.
I was staying with
my Mothers aunts
who lived in the country.
When I began to see
agen — a bit, in misty blurr,
they took me to
a sheep dog tirals.
Those dogs are amazeing,
knowing what to do
to make the sheep go
where they want.
I think Ill ask
for one — a dog I mean.
But Id have to have sheep
as well for what
woud it do without them?
Id like a dog of my own.
Therar dogs at home
for when therar shoots,
labradoors and things,
great big and black. Im
a bit afraid of them
tho theyre really nice
and kind but lick one so.
Id like a Shnow Sir.

Its a German dog,
a kind of terryer,
something like an Air Dale
but its whiteish-grey.
A very hairy face
so you cant see
its eyes or mouth.
Its strong and freindly
very Cuddly.
Ill ask my Father
Please may I have
a Shnow Sir, Now Sir?
But I know hell say
You'd have to look after him
all the time. He'd be
Your Responsibility.
And what would happen
when you're away at school?

Once when I was <u>very</u> small
I was in some thick old woods
with two other boys my age.
It was getting dark
and suddenly
from behind a tree
a huge dark shape
rushed out at us.
I rored and rored with fear
and I coud hear and listen to

my rore as if it had been
the rore of someone else.
The monster was just a dog,
but big, and black as night.
Later I heard it was a dog
of New Found Land
owned by someone
in the naybour hood.
The gentlest they are said to be.

Then one Christmas Holidays
there was a tremenjus snow.
The roads were blocked. No traffic
passed, and all was quiet and white.
I got permishon to tobbagon down
the empty main highway
where it sloped quite steaply to
a bridge across the river near
our home. It was a good long run,
the best Iv ever had and fast,
but safe becos I was the only thing
that moved. Agen and agen
for most of a long morning
I turdged up, slegded down,
enjoyed the cooling wind upon
my face, red tingling nose and ears,
and the smell of the forsty cold,
and happily thot of Christmas
soon to come, and then another year.

Freind of my Father
owns some fishing trawlers,
he says foreign vestments.
Vestments have to do with church
but why with fish and fishing?
Anyway, he took us
for a sail in one.
First time Id been
to sea (I think).
The up and down
when farther out
made me feel <u>kwisi</u>
tho I wasnt sick.
(not sure how to spel,
but word made me think of <u>kiwis</u>)
I havent seen all words
on paper yet, just know
what they mean
from how they sound.
Tho quite good at essays,
other kompusitions,
I dont spel well always.
But its not that
I dont try.

One of my aunts said
Ill be a worrier.
I said like William Wallace,

Cesar, Hanni Bald?
But she just smiled.

Our house is near a river.
From my bedroom I can see
the broad and rushing band of water
between its banks of woods.
When theres a moon
its like a trak of gleaming silver
in the night, and its I tell myself
a kind of magic spel
which makes me think of things,
the days and years to come,
adventure, fun, and what Ill be.
Im happy when Im home
and with my parents. I
can talk to them (some boys
say they cant) and tell them things
and what I think. They sometimes laff.
But then they listen too.

The rivers best in autumn and in spring.
Theyre times of change, becoming something else,
not like the long fixed times
of summer, winter when
its the same for months. Then
you feel stale, in heat or cold.
Altho in summer heats
I love biking up and down the Avenue.

It has big old lime trees at the sides.
They meet at the top to make a roof
of branches, and in summer, leaves.
There its shade, when out beyond
theres blazeing heat.
I like the cool air on my face
when I peddle fast. I like the
scent of lime flowers in the air,
while woodpidgeons burble throatilly
BrBr BrBr   Br   Br / BrBr BrBr   Br   Br.

I have a best freind of course,
at school, a boy my age.
We stay at each others houses
in the holidays, bike about
and have adventures on our own,
get taken by our parents here and there
farther afield, sometimes Abroad.
Once I was in Paris with my parents,
uncle and an aunt. I nearly didnt go
cos I was thot too young
to understand Abroad.
But my uncle said let him come
and well look after him.
It was different but after a while
the same. I didnt follow much
what people said (babbled in a rush)
tho Id started French. Later for me
therell be German, Latin, Greek

Im told. The things to eat were skrumshus
skrumptious, food and fruit, ice-cream.
We sailed on the Sen, went out to Ver Sigh,
huge long low and golden
in the sun with such a sweet
and marvlus scent whats that
I asked it was the blossoms
from the Orangerry down below.

Id mentioned Raymond my best freind
before I got distracted. Well,
he has one sister and he rags
and baits her all the time.
Its Konstant War
when theyre together.
I dont think its always funny.
For a girl, she doesnt seem so bad.
Iv said dyou <u>have</u> to fight
and bikker? Can it be necessary
<u>all</u> the time? Believe me he said
its necessary. Thats what girls are for.
Tho Id soonerve had a brother.

My Father likes to fish,
for salmon, sea trout, grilse and that.
Hes given me rods
and taut me how to cast
and fix the flies. I like all that
altho Iv not yet caut a thing
cept eels. But I like being

near the water and the sound it makes,
soothing and peaceful in the holidays.

Whatre you going to be
some Groan-Ups ask
when you leave school?
I know how to spel
Grown-Ups, but its my word
for them. How coud I say?
Im only eight. When old,
about fourteen, praps Ill know.
But I have to murmur some reply.
Iv always been told to be polite
to Groan-Ups and I try.
And usully they smile, look smug,
and I get rid of them that way.

Then there was my Adventure
(I spose you coud call it that).
It was at a school camp
held one summer. We
were organised with masters
rules and things — getting us
used to dissiplin. One night —
and it <u>was</u> night, and we were up
and out on an exercise
like soldjers, scouts and that.
We had to creap along

in single file and quiet
as mice. We were in trees,
bushes along the borders
of a stream. Coud hear it
rush far down below. I was creaping
as we should, like a Kommando
(faces blacked) in single line
when suddenly I wasnt creaping
any more but falling down
through branches, leaves,
right into space. I thot
Im now free-falling and
I wonder what Ill hit —
the stones, the rocks, the stream,
and praps Ill next be dead.
I wonder what thats like
praps Ill know next second
I thot as I fell and fell.
And then I landed — on my back.
I didnt hurt. I mustve
bounced down on some thick tussok
or deep soft grass it was to dark
to see but it was on dry land.
I heard an ankshuss voice
call from above
Stockney are you all right?
It was the chief master there
and I found I coud shout back

and reasshure. Some fellows
scrambled down to help me up the slope.
Then we went on.

Youll have gatherd Im
an Only Child. Groan-Ups
(its the kind of thing they say)
ask Woudntyouve liked to have
a Brother or a Sister? Most
multi-children I have known
say they envy <u>me</u>. I havent really
missed more of us yet.

We have a house at a sea resort
not far from home. We go there
in July-September
for longer or shorter spels
depending on weather, various things.
We know another family
who also have a house nearby.
We have a beach-hut for changeing,
bathing things, deck-chairs, and games.
On sunny mornings when we open up
were blasted with a smell of heat,
dry wood, and salt seaweedy tang.
Bathing things from over night are dry.
Sand on the floor hot to the feet.
Iv learned to swim a bit.

My Mother coaches me.
Shes very keen on swimming.
I like the side-stroke
and the back-stroke best.
The butterflys too hard as yet.
In the crawl, water gets up my nose.
I know it neednt
and its an important stroke.
Im working on it. Theres a master
whos a swimming coach at school.
The other family are our freinds.
The fathers in business, cant always
get down. Our mothers get on well.
Therar three boys, seventeen,
sixteen, twelve. Twelve
plays with me, looks after (!) me,
older but not <u>too</u> old to befreind
a Little One (!). Seventeen, sixteen
are hardly boys at all.
They have a sister, <u>older</u> <u>still</u>
praps <u>Twenty</u> (!!). She comes and goes.
Praps she has a Job or is
a Student. I think she has
a Boyfreind and he once appeared
at a weekend. With her three brothers too,
I spose shes used to boys.
I like her cos shes nice
and talks to me bout things

and I dont feel so small and young.
She has a car. Shes going to
be in a motor rally soon,
driving herself. That must be fun.
The big boys, Robert (seventeen)
and John, with Michael (twelve)
took us all sailing. Theyve
a big boat, two masts, a yawl.
We edgd out carefully from the port
on the auxiliary motor. That cut out
and there was a flurry with the sails.
Then they were up. They caut the wind
and we were off, to sail along
the coast, not too far out.
John told me to beware the boom.
It can swing over suddenly.
You wouldnt want to go home he laughed
without your head. But Robert
after a while said I coud hold
the tiller while we were on course.
'Just hold it steady'. I coud
feel it pulse and throb in my hand.
'Now you have sailed,' said Robert.
Another day we flew some model planes
from a stretch of open empty beach
towards the lighthouse. It stands
by the shore on rocks close to the sea.
So tall and white. I can see

its light flash in the dark.
Its not on an island like that one
in <u>To the Lighthouse</u>, which Iv read,
borrowd from my Fathers library.
I thot itud be adventure
but it wasnt tho theres this small boy
(James Ramsay, six at the start)
whos promised by his mother
to be rowed tomorrow if its fine
to the lighthouse seen far out
across the bay.
This visit doesnt happen now,
not until his mothers dead
and things have changed, and then
it does. Somethings compleated (praise
from his father) tho now in a way
too late. Its more about Grown-Up
(not here Groan-Up) life, about
things not turning out the way its hoped.
The fathers rather horrid,
tho he doesnt mean to be,
or think he is.
And Mrs Ramsays good and kind.
She tries to arrange the peoples lives
as she thinks best for them,
but can you? Then shes gone.

That was a good summer, by the sea,
tho Id come to feel uneasy
in myself, which Im not usully.
Made me feel 'Not yet old enough
for a man, nor young enough for a boy;
as a squash is before 'tis a peascod.'
Made me feel there is
another, older world than mine
out there I havent probed, full of
strange going-ons, relationships
which havent so far come my way.
Oh well, who knows,
years more I may be seventeen.

So Iv put down some thots.
All morning its rained and rained.
This isnt the essay now.
Ill have to wait for subjects
to be given out. But here maybe
theres stuff to draw on.
Now the suns come back
Ill see if I can go and fish
this afternoon. I hope
Ill get a catch.
The rain and then the brightness
may have stirred up the trout.

THE AHBUTSTER

'Looks fine for the garden party.'
'Ah but cats and dogs by noon.'
'Much better news today.'
'Ah but there will of course be war.'
Such friendly small talk,
commonplaces we allow ourselves
oil hinges of unlatching doors
through which, once opened,
heavier stuff may pass.
But the Ahbutster will not play.
There and then must register contempt
for easy optimisms,
fond romantic hopes.
Shows he's in step with perverse fate,
convinces, if, unwary,
you let argument ensue,
that he is in the right.
Always his battles are to be,
in his assurance, won.
Thus the slack, easy notions,
doubtless inertia-born,
are swept aside,
so that in desperate mental cast about
there's little left to seize on
for the next throw you'll hazard.
'Not a bad summer it has been.'
'Ah but the drought's set in.'
'A gallant blaze these last flowers make.'

'Ah but night frosts will finish them.'
'Election tomorrow. May not vote.'
'Ah but you must. Time this lot went.'
'Back hurts. Tomorrow see my leech.'
'Ah but yesterday's not too soon.'
'We're swallowed by developers.'
'Ah but neighbourhoods won't stand for it.'
'There is so little we can do.'
'Ah but the salient points elude.'

Ah,
but it may be his way
to caution, make alert to life
the weaker and the timid ones?

ODE TO NONFRIENDS

Now more and more these days of my age, I search
backwards to once, and think of the many there
    familiar, not as the closest
        friends, but a part of the spaces moved in.

Acquaintanceships at schools, from the working stretch
lived through, or distant relatives scarcely known.
    Are they alive still? Unlike many
        dear to me, recently too soon dying.

Whither such fringe folk? What did they all become?
Worthy careers or shallows and miseries?
    Marriage and children, singlenesses
        chosen, or by inertias happened?

We might have been close, given, or if we'd made,
some chance to know them. But there were others too
    who'd drawn and claimed us more, and answered
        our need for concord, the understanding.

Swellers of scenes, they're now without face in their
cosmetics years-spread, seen in a passing glance,
    or yet a half-suspicious eyeing:
        we alike blanked by our lifelong make-up.

To trace, to find them without excuse to give
might cause disquiet, a puzzlement to vex.
    Research, a devourer of time, to
        which there are now the more pressing dues owed.

And if we'd meet would they now know what to say
to us, or we to them, any more than then?
   Ineptly perhaps such a wond'ring
      gestures to fellowship long unbonded.

CHANGE

No card from her this Advent.
A letter came back: 'Gone Away'.
Family acquaintance. No romance.
Easier without that perhaps
to keep a friendship lasting.
Meetings once in a while.
The cards for Christmas with
four lines of added messages,
in latter days more prized.
I've written to ones now left
who still could know.
But we are in the isolation of old age
when communication becomes difficult,
or fails — shut out,
shut in, with just the past
for present, and the unknown.
Her people had leased a house
on the coast for the summer months,
and I was visiting one day.
I've found a snapshot I remembered.
She, a friend from their girls' school,
I in the middle sit
holding tennis racquets, smiling back
from merry, candid, laughing faces.
Happy smiles of whitest teeth,
in days before American 'Say Cheese',
that stretching of the lips,
had glazed the smile from eyes,

made one the camera-stilled beams.
We were at the start, fifteen or so,
that hopeful, carefree afternoon of youth,
of sunshine, tennis, ocean, sand,
preserving for me now
our look to those years ahead
which may have yielded, who can say,
attainments, flowered hopes, victories,
all time-levelled since.

I had gone home that night
in summer holidays from school
boyishly dreaming of what next
of interest, joys, in the weeks to come;
and screwed my racquet back into its press
until the tomorrows' games.

I wonder what, or if, I may hear yet.

WALKING IN THE GOLD

A time of blaze and gold
is the year's effulgent pomp
at fall of summer's yield,
aureate in festive pyre.
Loosed from a season's being,
on tree or bush,
the leaves, now each its own,
join in a latter merriment,
a hectic dance of death,
a sporting in the gusts.

They spiral down in vortices
of air to caress ground,
their new and last home here.
They swirl and rustle for a while,
now dry and clenched,
or curled as shaved tin,
rattling, tinkling, scrabbling,
buffeted in draughty coigns.
Rag-like, some stay,
persisting on,
ravaged, damp and flat
from winter rain and snows,
wanly to greet
their later selves
unpleating, soft and green
in the sister season;

birth, the sure renewing
programmed
for a time
yet.

And, somewhere at last,
disintegrating into earth or water, air,
in fires of autumn, spring,
all vanish
from our ken.

LEFT

We've seen them change
from the selves they were,
with illness, age,
or something happening
in the brain,
at body's breaking
move to another stage,
as these grasses, leaves
in gold and ochre fade.

Indifferent to that
which had absorbed them most,
forgetting what
was least forgettable,
to those near,
though love remains,
they are no longer they.

In us, who mourn such loss,
what yet may others see?

FALL DUSK

Like some Lowry man-figure
detached from its crowds,
in slant to wind's buffets,
pressing he heads
into October's dun.
A watcher might say
out there goes one
with purpose, a zest
born of the stirring
seasonal play,
for fresh enterprise;
what might be thought best
of aims he conceives.

But, that over, long gone,
he crunches dead leaves
just to pursue
the trailing end to the waiting,
now.

SOMEONE FOR ME?

They sit in chairs
(if well enough)
day-long
in the public rooms.
A visitor appears.
Heads turn.
'Someone for me?'
But no,
oftener for someone else,
and expectant, welcoming looks
fall into vacancy again.

Another.
Another day.
Another time.
Another one,
maybe.

Nurses, male attendants,
for the most part young,
smooth-skinned, muscular,
fair of flesh,
criss-cross the floors,
relentlessly kind,
no-nonsense cheerily brisk.
They loudly pronounce
their words as if
(since the old often are)

all must be deaf,
coaxing confidence
in those who have none.

This can be what is reached
in the end
for the constrained,
and they know
that at
the end
it could be worse.
But what is left of them
to last
longer?

Helpless, more or less,
despondent, living on
some others'
looks and words.

'IF IT'S FINE TOMORROW'

He had his first own bike when he was eight
or so. Struggled to balance. Rolled a yard
to come a cropper time and time on hard
ground. Knees bled till he held a poise, if late
it seemed. And then he flew, O Bliss, on air,
light as an angel, free for everywhere.

He pedalled up and down youth's avenues,
scenting linden flowers and joy, as if then
young Dominique, free yet of Madeleine,
home at Les Trembles, shimmering with far views
spinning under wheel, over valleys, now
dreaming what he'd be, heedless of just how.

He disappeared with then. Now other shades
and fisted shapes thrust up to cloud the gleam
of blue, green, gold with menace that would seem
to scrabble him as boyhood's clear sight fades.
The charmed dreamscape smears, broken is the line.
Mr. Ramsay says, 'But it won't be fine.'

The seemed, though fanned, flames down, a paling glow.
What may be glimpsed and held — the perch of land,
what mind can reach, the leaf that falls to hand,
the given, grown — will sum up what's to show
of how we are, have been, can be, to last
us through our time, consign us to the past.

People slip away, in death or by some
other change. People we knew, of a kind
with us, in a place when our paths entwined,
each part of each for a time. Have they come
to where their beliefs and hopes would have led,
or elsewhere, all unknowing, truly dead.

When nurtured longings, cherished, wilt, as vain,
and prayers-for seem not to have been allowed,
and the blood runs thinly, and we are bowed
by less sure strength, the vagaries of gain,
sund'rings of the self, the end here may fall,
with enwreathing dusk's loom, a stifling pall.

As years file off, verge on our closing age,
we shy at being marked out for the van
of those advancing up the line to man
positions set at forefront in the gage
with death. No turn back in that pressing on.
All things fragment around till all are gone.

And there is God, not to forget, who may
be busied somewhere in the vast extent
of his The Unimaginable, bent
on granting and denying, Yea or Nay,
constrained to necessitate with commands
some new and unforeseeable demands.

For a season, in each of us there's been,
perhaps, the striking of some spark, a blaze
before the dull again, before the haze
reclothe with scarves of doubt the failing scene.
And such transfiguration of the night
may beam a life to victory, if slight.

Walk in the woods. Now autumn, just before
its end. Most leaves are down, lie as deep beds
springy below foot still. The yellows, reds
moisten to damper grey. The green they wore
will come, but not from them. The flowering lime
will scent air of the living, for a time.

A TIME WITHOUT SHADOW

I have a photograph,
framed, set up,
of my parents in their orchard, she
nearer, he farther off,
among the fruit trees, touching plums
for ripeness, each preoccupied
and unaware of being stilled,
then, by my camera,
in a green world, breathing sunlight,
space and peace,
on one of August's later days.

They stand and move between the boughs,
pluck the odd fruit, table-soft,
from dusky Blue Czars, Green Gages,
blackish damsons, rusty-gold
Victorias slowly ripening
on trees, at walls. And a red plum
whose very redness looked unripe
but was not, its name forgotten
by me, or never known.

The parents are in casual clothes,
he in a light, short, linen coat,
she in a two-piece, long-loved suit
of worsted, medium brown, easy
for messing about at home.
They show absorption in
one area of their interests.
They are in their seventies here.

A part of their days together
at a time, I could think, without
shadow, without
what yet would be. Wanted or
unwanted, the past, the future
are not here.
My people are still here
as in their lives,
as I remember them.

At a winding of their garden
they'd made a herbaceous border
deep and rich with various plants
observant of the year's parades
in colour, fragrance. They were there,
often with one another, culling,
planting, slipping, separating, adding.

And I think of Pierre Auguste Renoir
and just such a border
starred with blossoms
in his painting 'Picking Flowers',
the title my reproduction bears,
alas. Weak name. No less in French,
and I hope not of his choosing
(biographies might settle this)
but some last-minute gallery's
'we'll have to call it something
for the catalogues'.

The two figures he painted,
the young girl and the older man,
are not *picking* flowers.
A gardener it would seem,
he's darkly trousered, waistcoated,
with long white shirtsleeves
and a yellowish straw hat.
Stooping, he points out a rose
to one of the family, or a guest,
from his employer's house.
Darkly also, fashionably clothed,
she stands quite near, attending,
or perhaps not, to what is said.
Her grey-gloved hands
are clasped in front of her.

Above knee-height their forms emerge,
assert their presence, from
this master's soft and fuzz-edged
greenery of leafy trees
and bushes, flowers.

A distant background landscape
spreads to blue-green woodlands
glimpsed, blue and white fields and sky.

What has been painted
stays, to last

longer.

IN THE FAR SPAN

It's been a long cast,
working our way through
this world's meted years,
doing what we'd found
we could do best,
or with what we could live,
trying to flower
by some achievement, glow
from a self-esteem;
best meriting the gift given,
framing as well
as we could devise,
requiting ones who'd earned
joy from our laurels.

It is being a long time,
and we work still at it,
for to stop would seem
a kind of dying.
And we hold to what remains
there in our sight,
and fear the yet unknown
we may not manage.

A NEW YEAR

Yet again.
For long we'd marked
this change,
rejoiced at
an end and a beginning,
induced thoughts
of what we'd achieve,
tried to compress strengths
as at the start
of a race.

Perhaps we'll succeed
this time,
make, accomplish
what we would,
and know fulfilment.

Far off, a wind
blows up in gusts
over the unseen land
in this, now January, night.

The bells and other clangours
jumble sound. Cracks
of fireworks splinter,
vein sky's black
with threads of yellow, red,
green, blue.

Ring out, ring out,
inspirit
if not too late
our flagging wills.

'WHAT, IN ILL THOUGHTS AGAIN?...'

November —
They've passed, a year more,
birthdays of ones close,
dead now, long missed. Mine too
in the month before.
Sagittarius, Scorpio.

Started January, then,
and February,
hardly spring in our
north-western quartersphere.
Weather waiting
to get better. Those who can
seeking places, now
or always,
in the sun.

A melancholy time
to appear,
in nature and
the human gyre,
at neither start
nor ending of
the calendar's
unheeding run.

Rejected, sometimes fingered, or
doubtingly shelved,
religions', astrology's,
psychologies' lore
will not spell
all people to themselves,
and some are
left as specimens unpinned,

remembering surprising things,
surprised at not remembering things,
having crouched for those decades
in some small nook
of the world's knowledge, trades,

with nothing left to build, rescind,
sensing a draw from distant parts,
a strong attraction, febrile, tense,
as if attached by tightening threads
of then-lived fervours, loves, to starts
in life that seemed to promise, once.
From cold to cold. —
Were summer seasons
sometimes radiant, gold?

And where, when
will the end fall
of a worldly span

THE OLD GAME

(With apologies to the admired Robert Lowell)

After some time away,
I — we — go up the coast
to the old
summer-cottage-and-farm country
of the Howells, the Winters,
the Winter-Howells,
the Starkers, the Streakers. My
ancestors!

Remember Great Aunt Thora Jarman,
with her flame hair,
and how she scorched her neighbors,
those Odoms?!

I recall a summer evening
— I was with another one —
when we went down
to that little movie-house
in Gurney's Cove
to see *Psycho* screening,
recent then.

                    Late night
I fetch my new, now wife a snack
from the fridge,
spumante wine, some cheese,
and *panettone* wrapped

in the surprisingly long-lasting
Italian tinfoil
that had packaged
Mother's body,
as the skunks scrabble
in the garbage cans
on the back porch.

What lies beyond women, wives,
the hand-cleansing salt scour
and sea fog of Maine;
beyond the core places,
Boston, the Middle West,
New York or Washington,
family and faces?

Only the need to know
what and who next, that changes lurk
in the years' corners
like pockets of grey smoke
gathering to spread.
What, for America,
for us?

We have more love to have
How to find our women,
how again be rid?

I have to be enslaved,
crave to be free!

Meantime, by day,
searching,
I drive these empty, fir-treed shores,
with the lone
abandoned houses, cliff
falling, graveyard waiting ...
Saddest those with flowers
long-shriveled, placed
by the infrequent visitor,
and no one near
to take them off.

At nights, we contend,
with our spirits, words,
and flesh, hour
by sleepless hour.

'I kissed thee ere ...'
No ...

        That
was someone else.

Dearest Lobster,
shall we to bed now?

IN THE PARK

The time's now mild
and warms her years.
She chances out,
sees where things grow.
Tries to forget
the winters' cold
with losses, fears,
in summer heat
from long ago.

OUT OF THE NIGHT

In cloaking dusk
lags the day's heat
dying in velvet.
Single cries
as of bird beast
in pain or fright
pierce the hush.
Was the shriek
their end?

A next dawn
filters in.
Mysteries of the dark
no longer proclaim.
What was heard
is not seen
in the dayscape
fashioning itself
again.

A VIEW OF OXFORD

My painting, ink and wash,
by P. La Cave,
is signed, and dated 1771.
He was from abroad,
perhaps the Netherlands.
Dates of his birth and death
conjectural.
He painted in England for a time,
some say with Morland.
Oxford's Ashmolean has a work;
could tell you more,
though little. Foreign:
not a household name.

Prevailingly thin grey,
with blue-green, light and darker,
yellows pale like sand,
the landscape breathes extent,
or early afternoon,
where the road falls
towards Hinksey's plain
in the middle distance,
luminous washed green.
Beyond, at the horizon's line,
diminished towers of Oxford
rise and string along
the background, merged with cloud.
Magdalen. New College.

Bodley. Sky-piercing St. Mary's.
The quite recent
Radcliffe Camera's dome.
Merton chapel's reassuring belfry.
And eventual Wren's octagonal,
ogival, latter-day attainment
of the gatehouse's upward thrust
at Christ Church, housing Tom.
Some woods stretch where
more Oxford buildings no doubt wedge,
in the town safeguarded
by two rivers (not in sight).
Faintest of blue hills, beyond,
meeting the sky.
Magdalen tower, then as now
cuts Oxford off
at that eastern quarter.
A mark not of questioning,
exclaiming — that
would be too unseemly — but
of what is there, exemplar
of proportion, authority,
and grace.
Beyond its bridge
lies something else.

Prominent, foreground, left,
each on a horse,
a farmer and his wife (say),

decently, prosperously clothed,
well-mounted, face
the downward road
of what is now Boar's Hill.
They seem to have paused
to catch the scene,
backs to the viewer.
The woman has a black
and wide-brimmed
shallow hat. Red-shawled,
she holds a basket,
sits sidesaddle on a bay,
a pannier at its flank.
The man's on a white mount.
Black hat, light-coloured coat.
A small and green-clad boy
stands by the rider's horse,
proffers a dark hat upside down
to catch alms should they drop.
The man ignores him, looks
ahead. Beside the boy
a small dog, spanielish,
patched white and fawn,
with no great expectancy,
routinely sniffs the ground.
Central, legs hidden
by the track's decline,
a second man drives
a bunching handful of sheep

(the farmer's or another's?).
His shirt, like the woman's shawl,
is red. Nearest foreground,
right, huddles a mass
of sandy dune-like mounds
topped with dark green clumps
which could be gorse.

Above the two on mounts
a tree (a pine, say) rears
at the painting's edge
to partway up the sky.
There, predominant,
softly looms
a billow of ash-hued
cumulo-nimbus, lit to the left,
pale cream on grey.
Over all the country
light and shadow seem
to hold or shift.

Something has been caught
and stilled, the historic place,
its townscape, landscape
on a bright and
shadow-scudding day.
The travellers to market
with their wares
are as unknown to the learned

there below, these (then)
five hundred years,
as those to them.
Two worlds within few miles
of one another,
coexisting, lasting.
Rural children
have grown up, learned
how to love and lose,
make do in childhood,
adulthood, and age.
And out of sight
down in the High
it will be quiet
in vacation time
this day in 1771,
with sounds
that make the silence
seem more to prevail:
the creaking cart,
the faster hurrying,
rattling carriage,
the scuffing sedan chair.
And the steps
of those on foot.
The dust. The mud.

And during term Oxford's
seething with eternal youth

encountering mentors' wisdom
long and sorely tried;
thick with scholarship
and churchmanship
and high statecraft
and lesser politics,
controlled manoeuvrings
to make or wreck.

Elsewhere the poet Gray
will die this July's end.
And farther to the east
at Salzburg Mozart
is fifteen,
his twenty-ninth symphony
yet to be. Gainsborough's
in his forty-fourth year,
Haydn's in his thirty-ninth,
Göthe in his twenty-second.
Constable is in his fifth.
Napoleon has one year more
than Wordsworth, Beethoven,
in their first.

And ahead lie
Newman, Gladstone, Ruskin,
Zuleika Dobson,
Jude the Obscure,

and more
in our centuries
unspeakable.

Sheltered between
the Chilterns
and the Cotswolds,
Oxford will stay
yet for a while,
enlarged, changed,
unchangeable.
From past centuries
its ethos soars
beyond those
with purpose
to transcend it. While
in the true progeny, it can
with its galvanic charge
exalt the selves they are.

Should I bequeath
my painting
to the Ashmole,
or gift it to
the Christ Church
Picture Gallery?

LIGHT IN THE AFTERNOON

Sun floods.

Through heavy leaves.
They shift and sibilate,
thinking of rain.

Through me,
with whiff of memory.
Scent of girl's sunned skin.
Scent of scent.
Scent of material, silk, cotton
(of death too,
that first acrid sweetness)
when lime-trees rustled
their scent in sweetness
and all seemed possible,
summer dust on the shoes.
Brides and roses.

Through the churchyard.

Not here, distant
(but near too),
where shining grass covers
modifications of matter.
Ones I knew.

On transmission of sunlight
I am with them again, mine,
I who knew them,
know them about me, for comfort,
still in the midst of things
among earth's living
in that human life we shared
for a time. We'd say
Does this add up to much?
Is that worth a try?
And smile over it.
Do you remember,
while you walk in sunshine,
but alone?

And I was there, once, young,
under the hot silk of the parasol,
and then to middle life, and age.

Through you, who knew me,
at moments when you remember
I live on a little there.
Watch with a love
not entirely disinterested.
For nothing is settled here,
though you may assume this.
And I cling
to my intermittent life in you,

my daughter's boy,
who knew me living,
as those I knew live yet in me,
and so beyond
to a point we do not know.

> I pass the churchyard
> (at an age when we begin
> to avert our eyes)
> to zest of mown grass,
> memories of journeys,
> settings out,
> returnings, opening leaves,
> and my dead branch.

I wait,
reluctant to die again with you,
as all die with the last
of those who knew them
(to enter another state).
Your next death sooner.

I know them about me
as sun floods today,
as it flooded my youth on earth,
about me fused as the sun
the wind rain tides which flow
through the livings' consciousness.

What is this I've heard,
or have I heard?,
carried in the sun,
in hardly stirring air,
in a voice of one
I knew, now
long ago.

Late afternoon
Sighs heat among the leaves,
denying rain
to the sun-filled air,
to heat, stilled
and still,
so that I've heard.

ALASTAIR MACDONALD was born and educated in the United Kingdom. He attended and has degrees from Aberdeen University, Christ Church, Oxford, and the Victoria University of Manchester. From 1955 to 1987 he was a member of the English Department of Memorial University, Newfoundland, where he is now a Professor Emeritus. Seven earlier books of poetry have been published: *Between Something and Something* (U.K., 1970), *Shape Enduring Mind* (U.S., 1974), *A Different Lens* (Newfoundland, 1981), *Towards the Mystery* (Newfoundland, 1985), *A Figure on the Move* (Newfoundland, 1991), *Landscapes of Time* (Newfoundland, 1994), and *If More Winters, or This the Last* (Newfoundland, 2003). His poems have been included also in many anthologies and magazines. He is a member of the Writers' Alliance of Newfoundland and Labrador, the League of Canadian Poets, and a former member of the Scottish Poetry Library Association.